I0419457

Quote Octopus
Melbourne, Victoria, 3053
Australia
www.quoteoctopus.com

In the early 1970s in Atlanta, I attended what had formerly been an all-white school but had become a black school after integration and white flight. Perhaps because of this, the teachers created a curriculum that included a focus on African American literature and history year-round, not just in February.

Natasha Trethewey

The peculiar fascination which the South held over my imagination and my limited capital decided me in favor of Atlanta University; so about the last of September I bade farewell to the friends and scenes of my boyhood and boarded a train for the South.

James Weldon Johnson

Thank you... 'Real Housewives of Atlanta,' for demonstrating a universal truth: Idiots like me will always watch idiots like you fight on TV. You will forever be in my TiVo.

Jimmy Fallon

I've actually performed at Gay Pride in Atlanta three times in my career. I've always had a large gay following, particularly in the lesbian community. I am grateful for that. To me, it means my music transcends categories. It also means that I'm a cute girl singing a rock song in an alto voice!

Jennifer Nettles

Medical knowledge and technical savvy are biodegradable. The sort of medicine that was practiced in Boston or New York or Atlanta fifty years ago would be as strange to a medical student or intern today as the ceremonial dance of a !Kung San tribe would seem to a rock festival audience in Hackensack.

Lewis Thomas

Coming from a small town it was tough to dream big. When I grew up in a small town in Georgia, my biggest dream was one day to be able to go to Atlanta.

Herschel Walker

I didn't dream about being a director. I didn't know I wanted to do something with film until the summer between my sophomore and junior years at Morris College in Atlanta, Georgia.

Spike Lee

I think as men begin to see things that address them, they will feel that they can relate. They can't relate to 'Basketball Wives,' 'Housewives of Atlanta.' I am not judging or criticizing those shows at all; what I am saying is the perspective is not necessarily the male perspective. 'Iyanla: Fix My Life' is inclusive of everyone.

Iyanla Vanzant

The Center for Disease Control started out as the malaria war control board based in Atlanta. Partly because the head of Coke had some people out to his plantation, and they got infected with malaria, and partly 'cause all the military recruits were coming down and having a higher fatality rate from malaria while training than in the field.

Bill Gates

Atlanta's my musical home. It really was the place where I really came alive.

John Mayer

I met Howard Zinn in 1961, my first year at Spelman College in Atlanta. He was the tall, rangy, good-looking professor that many of the girls at Spelman swooned over.

Alice Walker

Billy Graham is one of my great lifetime heroes. I think he epitomizes the essence of what a Christian leader should be. I have participated in some of his crusades a couple of times in Atlanta. I've seen the profound impact he's had on me personally, and on other people who were not Christians and accepted Christ as Savior.

Jimmy Carter

The best comedy audiences in the country and this is tried and true, I'm not just saying it, in my opinion are Boston, Atlanta, and Chicago.

Denis Leary

I teach a Bible study for homeless guys in downtown Atlanta every week. Been doing it for years. That's the guys I'd rather go talk to. I'd rather take my act outside the church.

Jeff Foxworthy

I can't be calm when I drive through sections of Atlanta that look more like Kinshasa, Democratic Republic of Congo, than America.

Cynthia McKinney

In my real life, both my bosses are gay. On the 'Real Housewives of Atlanta,' Andy Cohen is gay, everybody at Bravo is gay - we call them the gay mafia. Over at 'Glee' and 'The New Normal,' my boss Ryan Murphy is gay. On the show, my boss, played by Andrew Reynolds, is gay in real life. I'm surrounded by all my gay bosses.

NeNe Leakes

I think the saddest moment in my life just happened two months ago. My old nightclub partner passed away, Phil Erickson down in Atlanta. He - I owe him everything. He put me in the business and taught me about everything I know.

Dick Van Dyke

Once I went to bed in Orlando and I woke up in Atlanta. I have no idea how that happened.

A. J. McLean

I pointed out that the Atlanta Olympic bomber - as well as Timothy McVeigh and the people who protest against gay rights at military funerals - are Christians but we journalists don't identify them by their religion.

Juan Williams

But being on location and shooting, whether its in Puerto Rico or Atlanta, it always reminds me of how really cool my job can be. Interacting with the fans is one of the best parts of it.

Dwayne Johnson

Phil Niekro and his brother were pitching against each other in Atlanta. Their parents were sitting right behind home plate. I saw their folks more that day than they did the whole weekend.

Bob Uecker

It used to be that if you had a pretty good record, you could stop by a station in Little Rock or Atlanta and let the DJ listen to it. No way something like that can happen now.

Charley Pride

I think it's important for artists to work together. It's great for fans to see, like, Ludacris came out to our show in Atlanta and kinda made a surprise appearance there, it shows a mutual respect for what each other does.

Jason Aldean

Whether it's on the streets of Philadelphia or New York or Chicago or Atlanta or in a classroom in Newtown, Connecticut, people want to be safe.

Michael Nutter

It is a remarkable fact that smallpox, a scourge for thousands of years, has now vanished from the earth, except for two tiny vials, one locked in a highly secure facility at the Centers for Disease Control, in Atlanta, and another stored in a similarly secure vault in Siberia.

Michael Specter

I'm certainly thankful for what the Cubs did for me. I respect their organization. It's the same way with the Atlanta Braves, an awfully fine organization. I respect everybody who's down there, and that's still where I live today. But the Cardinals represent the best years of my career.

Bruce Sutter

The funny thing is, people only know me for having straight hair for work, but I live in Atlanta where it's hot and humid in the summertime. So when I'm home, I wear my hair natural. My hair is naturally curly; I don't have a relaxer.

Keshia Knight Pulliam

Atlanta is an incredibly cool city.

Andrew Lincoln

The Giants are looking for a trade but I don't think Atlanta wants to depart with a quality player.

Ron Fairly

I am happy with what I do. I'd love to be the manager of the Atlanta Braves, but they hired somebody this week. So I'll just have to be inordinately happy with one of the best jobs on the planet.

Robert Gibbs

The first time I was homeless was when I went to Atlanta. I was in a homeless shelter, then when I got a job I used to miss the curfew for the shelter. So I ended up sleeping outside in the streets.

Jay Electronica

A lot of things happened in a lot of places. And to see how well it was handled in Atlanta. There are a lot of reasons for Atlanta being a special town in the Civil Rights era.

Ivan Allen

There are three or four places in the country where people think of fashion: One is L.A., obviously. Another is New York. And I think Atlanta has to be in the top five cities where fashion is very big.

Cam Newton

My commitment to Atlanta and passion for sports and competition make this acquisition a perfect fit for me.

Arthur Blank

I feel like in Atlanta, if you were a female dancer, the more you can dance like the boys, the more respect you get. I was thrust into that kind of dance culture, and it was in my body.

Janina Gavankar

When we lived in a suburb of Atlanta, Georgia, my sister and I did a local play. My whole family got involved. My mom did the makeup. My sister and I were being homeschooled, and my parents wanted us to be socialized. We had a lot of fun with the other kids hanging out backstage.

Danielle Panabaker

I'm not in the clubs; I'm a homebody. I go out when I feel I have to for work or if there's a special function. You might catch me at the grocery store, but you won't see me out and about in Atlanta.

Keith Sweat

In Atlanta, with a large African-American population, Sosa is often considered a black man. In Miami and Los Angeles, with larger Hispanic populations, he is a Latino man, and the black label is rejected as robbing Hispanics of a hero.

Bill Dedman

In Atlanta, there's no limitation to where you can take your music. You can be as creative as you want to be.

Nayvadius Cash

I remember at the 1996 Olympics in Atlanta, Shaq always wanted me to show him steps over and over.

Hakeem Olajuwon

One of the greatest live recordings, I think, in the history of the world is Ray Charles in Atlanta... And they didn't even have a big mobile recording thing set up. The word on the street was they only had like two microphones, one for the band and one for him. Perfect recordings. I think it's mono.

Robbie Robertson

Standing on the podium at the 1996 Olympic Games in Atlanta and receiving a gold medal was the crowning jewel in a successful gymnastics career and, most certainly, the confirmation that my parents' sacrifices were not in vain.

Dominique Moceanu

I'll have to say winning the Olympic gold in Atlanta is a crowning achievement, along with the gold in the relay in the same games.

Donovan Bailey

Oscar Charleston was the Willie Mays of his day. Nobody ever played center field better than Willie Mays. Suppose they had never given Willie a chance, and we said that, would anybody believe there was a kid in Alabama who was that good? Or there was a black guy in Atlanta who might break Babe Ruth's home run record? No.

Monte Irvin

For the entire state of Georgia, having the premiere of Gone With the Wind on home ground was like winning the Battle of Atlanta 75 years late.

Anne Edwards

Many athletes competing in Atlanta wouldn't be here if it weren't for corporate support.

Mary Lou Retton

The Atlanta Braves are really all that our children know about this crazy baseball life, and we are so thankful for this upbringing for them.

Tim Hudson

There's not much to do in Atlanta, so the cast went to the gym together, went shopping together, and dinner was always a group thing. It's that whole summer-camp experience that making movies tends to be anyway.

Timothy Olyphant

My father was a promoter of Fresh Fest, and they needed an opening act. He got me a slot as a dancer. We tried it out the first time in Atlanta and the crowd went crazy. I was the opening clown.

Jermaine Dupri

Because I was in Atlanta, people didn't realize I'm one of the real forefathers in the game.

Jermaine Dupri

The city of Atlanta has always had a good spirit.

Ivan Allen

I don't have a permanent place where I live. I'm in Atlanta about six or seven months out of the year. I gave up on my place in New York. I don't have a place in L.A., but sometimes when I go there for the hiatus, I stay in temporary housing. It's all over the place, and I don't know where I live!

Brooke Elliott

It is in Virginia and Georgia that the war now rages and where it will continue; for at these points - Richmond and Atlanta - the enemy's main strength is concentrated.

Knute Nelson

Friday was Atlanta. That was fifteen bucks. Once a month, we made a six hundred mile trip from Indianapolis down to Atlanta, and at fifteen dollars, by the time you feed yourself and buy gasoline, you're minus about ten bucks.

Lou Thesz

Atlanta? I think it's the greatest city anywhere I know of.

Ivan Allen

Because I'm shooting 'The New Normal' and 'Real Housewives of Atlanta' at the same time, so my schedule is double. I leave one show and go and shoot the other. The cameras are with me for, like, every day of my life. So I'm extremely tired.

NeNe Leakes

If you don't like the way the Atlanta Braves are playing then you don't like baseball.

Chuck Tanner

I've always liked Atlanta. And not just for the strip clubs, but the shopping and the food.

Jon Stewart

A person like myself, born and raised in the inner city of Atlanta, Georgia, to lower-middle-class parents. But I had the opportunity to get an education, to go and earn a commission in the United States Army, to serve for 22 years, to lead men and women in combat.

Allen West

Also I'm a part of the people that I've worked with in baseball that have been so great to me, Mr. Earl Mann of Atlanta, who gave me my first baseball broadcasting job.

Ernie Harwell

That other saying, I'm a part of all that I have met, I think that would have to begin with my wonderful parents back in Atlanta when I was a youngster five years old I was tongue tied.

Ernie Harwell

I wasn't predicted to be anything. I just followed an inner spirit, and it put me in the right place and the right time. I didn't want to be the mayor of Atlanta. I didn't want to run for Congress. I didn't want to work for Martin Luther King Jr. I wanted to work close to him and be a writer and write about the movement.

Andrew Young

I'm not West Coast at all. I was born in Atlanta, but I grew up in Kentucky, outside of Lexington, in Winchester.

Tucker Max

I once sat next to Jim from Wild Kingdom on a flight from Atlanta. I find mentioning that opens a lot of doors.

Todd Barry

That's an economic development program in the metropolitan area. If they don't see that, and you don't get these things done, then you're competing with Texas and California and Atlanta; then you really have problems.

Richard M. Daley

I know the cadence of the language and the voice of Atlanta because I've lived here for so long.

Karin Slaughter

The president of the branch in Atlanta was a pastor of a church, the Reverend Sam Williams, a wonderful guy. He was middle-class and fairly militant for the time and place.

Julian Bond

I don't live in L.A. I actually live in Atlanta, Georgia. After I graduated from Spelman, I just stayed and never left. And I love it.

Keshia Knight Pulliam

I never thought I'd be on the cover of the 'Atlanta Journal' unless I killed someone.

Chris Robinson

It sounds pretentious to say I 'divide' my time, but when I am home, that usually means my house in Atlanta or my cabin in the North Georgia Mountains. The latter is where I do the majority of my writing.

Karin Slaughter

I feel like I'm doing something in Atlanta that nobody ever did as far as rap. If it happens to end up on the top 40 or the pop charts, it doesn't mean I meant to go pop. It's just where the music took me. It started at the bottom, and it rises.

Nayvadius Cash

I became a novelist because of 'Gone With the Wind,' or more precisely, my mother raised me up to be a 'Southern' novelist, with a strong emphasis on the word 'Southern' because 'Gone With the Wind' set my mother's imagination ablaze when she was a young girl growing up in Atlanta.

Pat Conroy

I was a huge ham in school in Atlanta.

Hannah Storm

I always wondered how it would be to put on a Braves uniform and play in Atlanta.

Tim Hudson

I'm excited about being here in an organization that I grew up rooting for... I'm excited about being an Atlanta Brave and pitching in Game 1.

Tim Hudson

The very first time I was on a car in Atlanta, I saw the conductor - all conductors are white - ask a Negro woman to get up and take a seat farther back in order to make a place for a white man. I have also seen white men requested to leave the Negro section of the car.

Ray Stannard Baker

I was trying to land an 18-year-old strapping first baseman from Blanco, Texas, population 200. His name was Willie Upshaw. It turned out there were only three scouts who knew about Willie - Dave Yocum and I working for the Yankees, and Al LaMacchia from the Atlanta Braves.

Pat Gillick

Los Angeles, Houston, Denver, Atlanta: those are all cities that really didn't get big, didn't hit their stride until the 20th century.

Paul Goldberger

I grew up in the suburbs north of Atlanta. I had an amazing childhood, and I still go back to my home in Atlanta often.

Devon Werkheiser

At St. Francis de Sales in Atlanta, we do not have an organ. We do not have rehearsals during the week. We do not have a professional choir.

Richard Morris

I was a huge fan of Bobby Cox, a huge fan of Chipper Jones and John Smoltz. And just those guys, I grew up watching those guys and often wondered early on in my career if I would ever have the chance to play for the Atlanta Braves, and there it was. God kind of answered my prayers.

Tim Hudson

When I was traded from the Oakland A's to the Atlanta Braves before the 2005 season, a childhood dream was realized. I grew up a Braves fan just a few hours south of Atlanta, and it was hard for me to believe that I was going to actually play for the Atlanta Braves and legendary manager Bobby Cox.

Tim Hudson

I worked with Snoop, but I would love to work with him again, but DMX... I would love to work with him as well... I met him in Atlanta; I went to one of his concerts; I would love to do a song with him. I respect him and really like his music.

Bow Wow

I went down and played with Magic Johnson at his all-star game in Atlanta. I remember Magic stopped the game and said, 'We need you here with us in L.A.'

Jayson Williams

My first day as a manager was at Digital Equipment in Atlanta. I was a sales rep. I was promoted from among my peers, so one day I was a peer, and the next day I was their boss.

Carol Bartz

As I got older, I'd say probably when I got to, like, seventh or eighth grade, I was living in Atlanta, Georgia at the time, and I went for an open call for an agent, a local agent out there, a woman named Joy Purvis, and she ended up picking me up.

David Lambert

I always looked up to great actors and great films. A lot of my family would be like, 'Come on, you should get into these plays that are going on.' I'm like, 'Nah, nah, music's my thing.' I just fell into it. I moved to Atlanta, got with an agency out there, started doing little voiceover commercials, and it started getting kind of fun.

Jacob Latimore

My first novel, 'Leaving Atlanta,' took at look at my hometown in the late 1970s, when the city was terrorized by a serial murderer that left at least 29 African-American children dead.

Tayari Jones

Billy Barnes signed me and got me my first role in an interracial love story filmed in Atlanta called 'Together For Days' with Clifton Davis. My mother thinks it was my best work. You cannot find a copy of it.

Lois Chiles

I grew up kind of in the country, in western Georgia. And then I moved a lot closer to Atlanta, and I started doing plays, and when I started doing film, I think I really started to love it.

Morgan Saylor

My wife and I came to Canada for the 1994 Commonwealth Games and we really liked the B.C. lifestyle and environment. The following year we applied to become permanent residents. We moved here in 1996 after the Atlanta Olympics.

Jonathan Brown

In 2001, I moved from Philly to Atlanta, where I lived for six years. I had never lived anywhere but Philly, and you can imagine the culture shock; the Civil War seeps into daily life and conversation down South in a way it never does up North.

Karen Abbott

I lived in Atlanta for a couple of years while getting my masters at Georgia State. I thought I hated it at the time, but I've been back a couple of times since, and there's no place I've lived to which returning is so much like visiting a place I only remember from my dreams.

David Liss

We don't have any CGI with any of the car stuff. I think it's a real experience when you see this car going through really fast really wild and you see me driving a lot of the times and also a big chase in downtown Atlanta. It's just incredible.

Sean William Scott

The best food I've had was actually in catering at 'Single Ladies.' It's insane. I can't live in Atlanta. In fact, even if I'm offered, I'm not sure I could come back for another six months, because I'll just be fat.

Ricky Whittle